# This Is An Orchestra

By

Elsa Z. Posell

*Illustrated With Over Thirty Photographs*

HOUGHTON MIFFLIN COMPANY · BOSTON

The Riverside Press Cambridge

# ACKNOWLEDGMENTS

To THE many friends and colleagues who have given generously of their time and effort in the preparation of this book, my most sincere thanks and appreciation. Foremost among these are George H. L. Smith, program annotator of the Cleveland Orchestra; Margaret Clark, head of the Children's Room of the Cleveland Public Library; Elizabeth Briggs, Director of Work with Children, Cleveland Public Library; Harriet G. Long, Associate Professor in Children's Literature, Library School of Western Reserve University; and Charles Howard Allen, Jr., Editor of Western Reserve University Press.

I am especially grateful to Carl J. Vosburgh, manager of the Cleveland Orchestra, for his particular cooperation; to Mrs. Edward Howey Brown, former School Librarian of the Cleveland Public Library; to Mary Williams Rautenberg, formerly of the Music Department, Vassar College; and to Mrs. Alfred R. Willard. Special thanks are due the libraries and staffs at Oberlin College and the Fine Arts Division of the Cleveland Public Library; the many members of the Cleveland Orchestra for their technical and practical advice; and last but not least, my own children and husband, without whose help and experience this book could not possibly have been written.

*Tenth Printing* R

# CONTENTS

# THE CLEVELAND ORCHESTRA

## GEORGE SZELL, *Conductor*

---

### *FIFTEENTH PROGRAM*

THURSDAY EVENING, JANUARY 27, 1949, *at 8:30 o'clock*
SATURDAY EVENING, JANUARY 29, 1949. *at 8:30 o'clock*

---

ZINO FRANCESCATTI, *Violin*

Symphony in G major, "Oxford," No. 92          Haydn

    Adagio; Allegro spiritoso
    Adagio
    Menuetto; Trio
    Presto

Concerto for Violin and Orchestra No. 3 in B      Saint-Saëns
   minor, Op. 61

    Allegro non troppo
    Andantino quasi allegretto
    Molto moderato e maestoso; Allegro non troppo

INTERMISSION

Symphony No. 2 in C major, Op. 61          Schumann

    Sostenuto assai; Allegro ma non troppo
    Scherzo: Allegro vivace; Trio (I); Trio (II)
    Adagio espressivo
    Allegro molto vivace

# 1

# Waiting for the Orchestra
# to Start

It is only ten minutes past eight and the concert won't start until eight-thirty, but already the Music Hall is almost full. Ushers in the aisles walk back and forth showing people to their seats. The huge stage is empty. To one side the harp gleams in the bright light. The double basses stand out in comparison to the tall stools near them. The stillness of the empty stage is interrupted as men begin to appear from each wing carrying their instruments. They make an impressive picture in their formal full dress clothes or "tails," as they call them. Their instruments are bright, showing various colors of wood, and the brasses gleam and shine in the brilliant light.

The Hall is full of sound, the high notes of the piccolo, the trumpet interrupting its song with a loud melodic tune and the bassoon singing away in short low tones, the strings each playing his own selection.

The concertmaster has now come to the stage and

with a few short taps with his bow over his music stand, he silences the orchestra. The oboe now sounds the A for the men to tune their instruments.

Again silence that is broken by a burst of applause as the conductor steps from the wings, and the concert is about to begin.

This is what most people see and hear when they go to a concert. Few think of all the thought, planning, and hard work that was necessary beforehand.

In order to play music, an orchestra must have many different instruments just as an artist needs different paints to paint a picture. The conductor, who is responsible for planning the programs, knows which instruments he will need by referring to the conductor's score. He consults this score in the same way as a play director would consult the play he was to produce or direct. In it the play director will find a list of players or characters and their parts, just as the conductor will find from the score the instruments needed for a certain composition and the part that each instrument will play.

When a composer has an idea for a composition, he writes it down just as a poet would jot down the poem he has created. He probably plays it over on the piano several times and then puts it on paper so that it can be played by a pianist. If he plans to have his composition played by an orchestra, he begins over again, using the melodies he has already written for the piano. Because the composer knows the instruments and how they sound, he assigns parts of his melodies to different ones, using

GEORGE SZELL, Conductor of the Cleveland Orchestra, at rehearsal.

them in as many combinations as he feels will make his composition sound best when played by an orchestra. The parts he has given to the instruments of the orchestra are written on large sheets of ruled music paper on different staves or lines, showing exactly what notes each instrument plays and when each instrumental voice enters. This, then, is the conductor's score.

For the sake of convenience, it is customary to group the instruments on the score page in the following order: first at the top are the woodwinds, next comes the brass family, followed by the percussion instruments, with the string family last.

The parts for the different instruments are copied from the score so that each player can have his own. Some instruments have more to play than others, just as in a play some characters have bigger roles than others and, therefore, have more to say.

The score itself is for the conductor. On the first page are listed all the instruments he will need to play the composition. Most scores call for an orchestra using all the instruments in the orchestra families. There are, however, some scores that omit certain instruments or call for others that are not regular members of the symphony orchestra. When a score requires particular instruments such as the saxophone, the mandolin, or other instruments for special effects, an extra person playing that instrument must be found for the performance.

From the score the conductor can read each player's part and can tell when any of the players make mistakes

# Die Meistersinger von Nürnberg.

## Vorspiel.

Richard Wagner.

ich u. Druck von B. Schott's Söhne in Mainz.

or do not start playing in the right place. Players may and do take their individual parts home to practice before rehearsing with the whole orchestra. During rehearsals the conductor carefully supervises each man's playing and blends and balances all the different instrumental voices to produce the best possible performance of the composition. The finished concert or recording is the result of days of practice and hard work on the part of the conductor and the members of the orchestra.

Except for a few minor changes, the seating plans of most symphony orchestras are basically alike. The entire front of the orchestra is occupied by the violin, viola, and violoncello players. The concertmaster sits at the very first stand of first violins to the left of the conductor. In the center of the stage behind the strings are the woodwinds, and, behind them, the brass and percussion instruments. The string basses are usually at the very back of all the other instruments, either to one side or right across the middle of the stage. The harp is generally placed either at the extreme left or right of the stage.

The name of each player is usually listed in the program under the instrument he plays. From this listing it is evident that the violins outnumber any other instrument in the orchestra and that they are divided into two sections, called first and second violins. They are so divided to permit the first violins to play one part, while the second violins play another. This gives more contrast to the string section and better shading and coloring to the orchestra. The modern large symphony orchestra consists of approximately 100 players and the string sections are divided as follows: 18-20 first violins, 16-18 second violins, 12-14 violas, 10-12 cellos, 8-10 basses. This adds up to approximately 70 string players which is the largest percentage of players in the orchestra. The remaining players are members of the woodwind, brass and percussion sections.

In the dim light of the hall only the stage is bright. The audience is silent, sitting back with eyes closed or leaning forward to watch the performers as they play. How well the notes from the various instruments blend together and what a thrill it is to hear a solo by an instrument, and to recognize it as the French horn, or the clarinet, or the bassoon! How mellow and sweet the horn can sound, how melancholy the clarinet is at times!

The end of the last number of the program is followed by a thunderous applause. Many times the conductor is recalled to the stage to share with his orchestra the long loud clapping which is the way audiences have of showing their appreciation for a fine concert.

# Seating plan for an orchestra

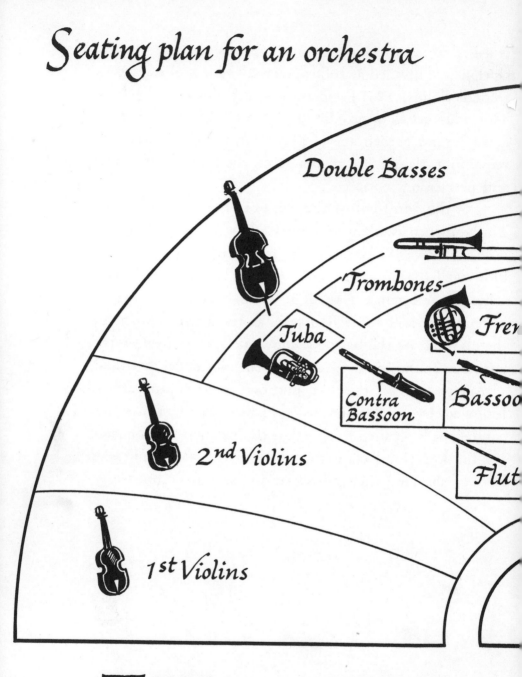

Double Basses

Trombones

Tuba

French

Contra Bassoon

Bassoo

2nd Violins

Flut

1st Violins

**THIS** is one of several seating p
usually determines the seating of t
upon the acoustics of the hall.

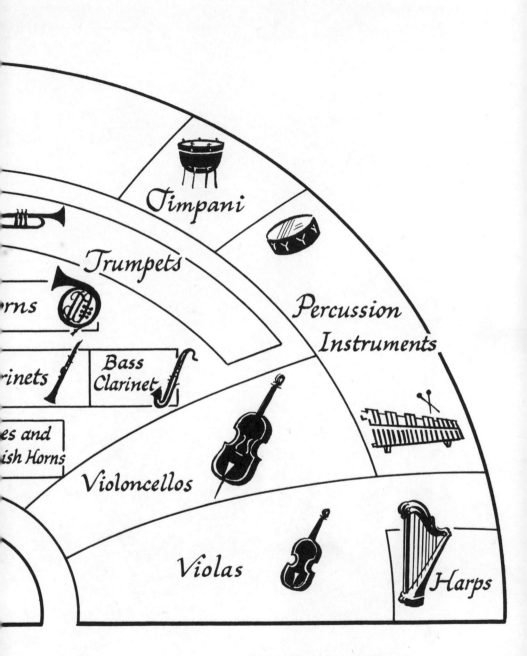

Timpani

Trumpets

rns

Percussion
Instruments

rinets

Bass
Clarinet

es and
ish Horns

Violoncellos

Violas

Harps

d in different orchestras. The conductor
estra but sometimes it is dependent

# 2

# Instruments of the Orchestra

AN ORCHESTRA is made up of many different instruments. They all vary in shape, size, and the way in which they are played. Some instruments are played by drawing a bow across a set of strings, some produce tone when they are struck, shaken, or rubbed, and others must be blown into. The material of which they are made differs too. Some are made of metal, others of wood.

These instruments that make up the modern symphony orchestra are used very much in the same manner as an artist would use his different paints to paint a picture. Each instrument, no matter how large or small, has a voice of its own. By combining the voices of the various instruments, and arranging them so that each will sound to best advantage, the composer is able to color his composition, to paint a musical picture and to create the moods and emotions we experience when listening to an orchestral concert.

Because of similarities either in the manner of playing or in the materials of which they are made, instruments are divided into groups or families. There is always a definite relationship between instruments within one group or family. The instrument families are:

1. The Strings
2. The Woodwinds
3. The Brass
4. The Percussion

## THE STRING FAMILY

This family consists of four instruments. They are: the violin, the viola, the violoncello, or 'cello, and the double-bass or contra bass or string bass. Instruments in this group have more in common with each other than do those in any other family groups. Though different in size, they resemble one another very much. They are all made of wood, as if from the same pattern, but in four different sizes, starting with the smallest, the violin, and ending with the largest of the four, the string bass. Their tone is produced by playing a bow across a set of four strings. Sometimes the strings are plucked with the fingers. This is called pizzicato, an Italian word meaning to pinch or snap with the fingers. This group of instruments is descended from the ancient viol family, which included besides the viol such instruments as the viola d'amore, the viola da braccio, and the viola da gamba.

The importance of the strings in the orchestra cannot be overestimated. The singing qualities of the violin and the violoncello make it possible for them to carry the principal melody either alone or reinforced by the wind instruments. The string choir supplies a richness, a depth and softness that cannot be matched by any other group of instruments. Composers often write for strings alone because the tonal effects produced by a large body of stringed instruments can be extremely varied and are rarely monotonous.

# THE VIOLIN

The violin is the smallest instrument of the string family. As the soprano voice it can produce the highest notes of all the strings. Its four strings are tuned to the tones of G, D, A, and E. It is the G string that gives the violin its deepest tones while the E string gives it its most brilliant and highest ones.

Small as the violin may seem, it is made up of about 70 different parts. Of these, 57 are used in the construction of the instrument itself and 13 are parts that are removable, such as the strings, the bridge, the tail piece, pegs, and several other parts. Violins are made of several kinds of wood. The back, neck, scroll, ribs, and bridge

THE VIOLIN

are usually maple. Spruce is used for the belly or top, while the block linings, bass bar, and sound post inside are of pine. Ebony is used for the tail piece, fingerboard, pegs, and nut. The strings are tightened by means of pegs set in the scroll of the instrument and are tuned in fifths. All parts of the violin are held together only with glue. No nails or screws of any kind are used. In all the instruments of the string family, the wood used and the construction are the same.

The bow, an important element in playing these instruments, can be traced to the hunting bow. Since then, it has gone through many stages of development, but it was François Tourte (1747-1835), a famous French bow maker, who was responsible for the modern bow. The shape and curve of the stick, the length and weight of the bow and all its trimmings are the product of his experimentation, hard work, and ingenuity.

. The violin bow is usually made of pernambuco wood, which comes from Brazil. The hair used for the bow comes from the tail of a horse and is always bleached white before it is set into the bow. When the bow hair becomes slippery, players rub rosin on it to keep the bow from sliding and to help it grip the strings.

# THE VIOLA

The viola, which is next in size to the violin, is only slightly larger, and its strings are a bit thicker and longer. It is played in much the same manner as the violin. The strings are tuned in fifths to C, G, D, and A. Music for the viola is written in the alto and treble or G clef, and the instrument is often referred to as the alto or tenor voice in the orchestra.

The tone of the viola is not as brilliant as that of the violin. It is rather a veiled tone and is often used by composers to describe gloom and melancholy. Violas differ slightly in size as do violins. Some of the largest violas were made by Gasparo da Salo, one of the greatest string instrument makers. The supposed standard size of the viola is only about a seventh larger than the standard violin.

THE VIOLA

# THE VIOLONCELLO

This instrument is the third in size in the string family. Like the viola, it has four strings tuned to C, G, D, and A, but they sound an octave lower than those of the viola. The ancester of the violoncello, or 'cello as it is popularly called, is the viola da gamba. It is a much larger instrument than either the violin or the viola and is held between the knees of the player and supported by a peg which is inserted in the bottom of the instrument and which rests on the floor. Violoncello in Italian means "little bass."

There are usually 8 to 12 'cellos in the average symphony orchestra and composers write more freely for the 'cello than they do for the viola. The 'cello can play lower than the viola, yet reach higher notes with greater brilliance. Composers use this instrument to express many different colors and moods. The playing range of the 'cello is about four octaves and music for it is written in the bass, the tenor, and the treble clefs.

The violoncello, though similar to the violin and the viola in looks, is proportioned rather differently. The ribs of this instrument are much higher in relationship to its body than are those of the violin and the viola.

THE VIOLONCELLO

# THE DOUBLE BASS

The double bass (or string bass, or contra bass) is the largest instrument of the string family. It is about six feet high and the player usually has to stand up or sit on a high stool to play it. In most cases the instrument is much taller than the player himself. It is the bass voice of the orchestra and plays the lowest notes in the string family. This instrument, with its flat back, high bridge, and sloping shoulders, resembles its ancestor, the basse de viole of the older family of viols. The strings are quite thick and are tuned in fourths to E, A, D, and G. Music for the double bass is written in the F or bass clef and sounds an octave lower than it is written. Modern composers have also written for it in both the tenor and the treble clefs like the 'cello. It, too, is supported by a peg which is inserted in the bottom of the bass and which rests on the floor.

Double basses in the orchestra are used mostly for background and strength, and to express great emotions of stress and moods of gloom and foreboding. Solos are rarely heard on this instrument, though modern composers occasionally write a short solo passage for it in the orchestra. There are between 8 and 10 basses in the average large orchestra. The bow of the double bass is heavier and shorter than that of the 'cello and the tone, especially when blended with the 'cellos, is deep and rich.

THE DOUBLE BASS

# THE HARP

The harp is one of the most ancient of instruments. The Bible speaks of its existence and pictures of it are found on Greek vases many centuries old. During its long history it has undergone many changes in shape, size, and the number of strings used. In 1809 Sebastian Erard, a Frenchman, devised a system of pedals which would permit the player to play in any key. It was not, however, until many years later that the harp became a member of the symphony orchestra.

The modern harp has 47 strings and 7 pedals. The 12 longest strings are made of wire, the rest are made of sheep gut. Nylon harp strings are also being used now by many harpists. Only four fingers of each hand are used to pluck the strings. The little finger is never used since it is too short.

The harpist is able to play in any key and to change from one key to another by using the 7 pedals which are worked with the feet. The pedals are named after the letters of the scale (A, B, C, D, E, F, G) and control the strings of the same name. The D pedal controls all the D strings, the C pedal, the C strings, and so on. Music for the harp is written on two staves, similar to that of the piano.

Harp strings are made in different colors. The C strings are green, the F strings are a purplish blue, and, with the exception of the 12 large wire strings, all the rest are red. There are still some harpists who have not accepted the color change in harp strings and use red

C strings, blue-purple F strings, and white for the remainder. The strings are different in color to help the harpist find the notes quicker. The harp is the largest instrument in the orchestra and is very beautiful to look at as well as to listen to.

In an orchestra there is usually only one harpist but many orchestras employ two regularly since there are many works in which there are parts for two harps. Though technically a string instrument, it is not considered part of the string family since it is not played with a bow and is not constructed like any other instrument in that family.

THE HARP

# THE WOODWIND FAMILY

The woodwind family consists of the flute and piccolo, the oboe and English horn, the clarinet and bass clarinet, and the bassoon and contra-bassoon. These instruments are much alike because each is constructed of a hollow tube which must be blown into to produce sound. Originally all of these instruments were made of wood, and now all but the flute and piccolo and sometimes the clarinet are still made of wood. Some of the instruments of this family are played by means of either a single or double reed mouthpiece. This is placed between the player's lips and when blown into it sets the air column in motion in the instrument. Clarinets and saxophones use a single reed mouthpiece and the oboe, English horn, bassoon, and contra-bassoon use a double reed. The reed is made of the outside layer of a certain grass grown in southern Europe. The flute does not use a reed at all, but its tone is produced by the player's blowing directly into an opening in the instrument.

In all wind instruments the tone is produced by a column of air which is set in motion by the player, and the pitch is controlled by a series of holes, bored at certain distances. These holes are opened or closed by a system of padded keys which lengthens or shortens the air chamber within the instrument.

Some wind and brass instruments are pitched in various keys and are called transposing instruments. For instance, a trumpet in B flat or a clarinet in A, or a horn in F are transposing instruments. This means that the

THE OBOE FAMILY    English Horn, Oboe d'Amore, Oboe.

notes they play do not sound as they are written. For example, the note C when played on the B flat trumpet, will sound B flat or one whole tone lower than C. The same note (C) will sound A on the A clarinet or one and a half tones lower than C. However, a trumpet in C or a horn in C will sound as written (non-transposing). The transposing instruments are the English horn, clarinet, trumpet, horn, and tuba. Some players learn to transpose on their instruments by counting the distance or intervals between notes and some transpose by reading their part in a different clef.

# THE FLUTE

This instrument, like the harp, has been in existence longer than many other instruments in the orchestra today. The flute, which used to be made of wood, is now made of silver and consists of three hollow tubes all fitted together to form one long tube. The first part of this tube is called the head and contains the opening into which the player blows to produce sound. The other two sections contain the intricate system of holes and keys which the player fingers.

Like other instruments, the flute, too, went through many changes before it became the perfect instrument it is today. Theobold Boehm, a German flutist, spent many years working on the flute, trying to develop a

THE FLUTE

system which would permit the player to play all the notes in the chromatic scale. At this time, the flute had a very inadequate system of mechanical keys or levers. By 1852 Boehm perfected a keyed flute with much greater facility, purer intonation, fuller tone, and greater range than it had had before.

The flute is one of the most important members of the orchestra, and composers often write lyrical solo passages for it. Though the tone sounds somewhat hollow in the lower register, it is mellow and sweet in the middle, and strikingly brilliant in the high register. There are usually three flute players in the average orchestra. The third player often plays the piccolo in addition to the flute. This is called "doubling" on an instrument.

# THE PICCOLO

"Piccolo" in Italian means small or diminutive, and this instrument, though built almost exactly like the flute, is only about half its size. Instead of being in three sections or parts, it is made up of only two sections. The piccolo is pitched an octave higher than the flute. It has a very shrill, piercing sound in the high register and has none of the flute's sweetness and mellowness. One of the most important uses for the piccolo is to add color and brilliance to the woodwind section. Every

THE PICCOLO

flute player has at some time also played the piccolo. In many orchestras a flute player doubles in both flute and piccolo, though most of our larger symphony orchestras have one member of the flute section who devotes most of his time to the piccolo.

# THE OBOE

The oboe is a double reed instrument made of wood. It is only a little over two feet long, tube-shaped almost to the end, where it becomes wider, like a bell. At the thin end of the instrument there is a small metal tube into which the double reed mouthpiece is placed. The reeds are held together by means of thin but strong string. The player blows into this mouthpiece to produce sound in the instrument. Since it requires little air to produce a tone, the player must at times withhold his breath to be

THE OBOE

sure that he does not blow too hard. This is one of the reasons why the oboe is such a difficult instrument to play.

The oboe is a non-transposing instrument, which means that the notes it plays sound exactly as they are written. Pitch is controlled by a system of keys used to open and close the holes pierced in the tube. Its tone is penetrating, plaintive, and at times nasal. It is often used to play solo parts in the orchestra, besides, of course, to blend harmoniously with the rest of the woodwind choir.

The oboe sounds the A which is used to tune all the instruments in the orchestra.

# THE ENGLISH HORN

This instrument is most unlike its name, being neither English nor a horn in the true sense of the word. It, too, is a double reed instrument and resembles the oboe, though it is one and one half times longer and considerably wider. It is made of a round tube of very hard wood with holes pierced at certain distances along its length. A system of padded keys which opens or closes holes in the body of the instrument changes or regulates the pitch. It is pitched five tones lower than the oboe, and the method of playing and fingering is similar. The round shaped bell at the end of the tube is responsible

THE ENGLISH HORN

for its resonant and unique tone. The English horn player, too, must learn to control his breathing. The tone of this instrument is rich and mellow with a hint of sadness always to be found in it.

The oboe and English horn must be made of hard wood so that they will not warp or crack. Numerous experiments at making these instruments of materials other than wood have proven unsatisfactory. In most orchestras there are three oboe players, the third usually doubling on the English horn. The larger orchestras, however, employ an English horn player who devotes himself mainly to that instrument.

# THE CLARINET

The clarinet is a single reed instrument. Though almost always made of wood, many clarinets made of metal are now used in schools and bands. Like the oboe, it is a tube made of ebony about two feet long, expanding slightly into a bell shape at one end. It has the greatest range of all the woodwind instruments and there is great variety in the quality of its tones in the different registers. The low notes of the clarinet are mellow and extremely pleasant. In the middle register its tones are very clear and sweet, but it is not until we hear the clarinet in the high register that we realize how brilliantly the instrument can play. We also find it a little shrill in this register.

The ancestry of this instrument can be traced back to the Greeks, but it was not until the late seventeenth century that Johann Christoph Denner, an instrument maker, improved it to the point where it can be recognized as the modern clarinet. Theobold Boehm, who perfected the flute, applied his system of keys to the clarinet, making it the lovely instrument used in the modern symphony orchestra today.

Most clarinets in the orchestra are pitched in B flat or A. Occasionally certain scores call for higher clarinets pitched in D or E flat.

THE CLARINET

# THE BASS CLARINET

The bass clarinet is twice as long as the ordinary B-flat or A clarinet. It sounds an octave lower in pitch and also uses a single reed. As in the other clarinets, the pitch is controlled by the player's fingers operating padded metal keys fitting closely over the holes. The tone quality of the bass clarinet is deep, rich, and often melancholy. Because of the turned up metal bell, it somewhat resembles the saxophone in appearance. A peg inserted in the

THE BASS CLARINET

bell of the instrument rests on the floor supporting it while it is being played.

Three clarinets are used in a symphony orchestra, the third player doubling on the bass clarinet unless four clarinets are used. Then one player usually devotes himself principally to the bass clarinet.

# THE BASSOON

This is a double reed instrument and, with the exception of the contra-bassoon, is capable of playing the lowest notes in the woodwind family. The Italian name for this instrument is "Fagotto," which means a bundle of sticks. The bassoon consists of a wooden tube about eight feet long which, when doubled for the sake of convenience, looks like a bundle of sticks and so received the Italian name it now bears. A strong cord around the player's neck helps support the instrument and gives him more freedom to manipulate the keys.

At one end of the instrument there is a curved metal tube which holds the double reed mouthpiece. Curly maple or rosewood is most often used in making bassoons. The keys are usually made of silver. Though the bassoon is often called the clown of the orchestra, it is capable of producing beautiful mellow tones, particularly in the upper register, and often is called upon to play long melancholy passages.

In most symphony orchestras three bassoons are used, the third player often doubling on the contra-bassoon. In the larger orchestras four bassoon players are used and the contra-bassoon player usually devotes himself mainly to that instrument.

THE BASSOON

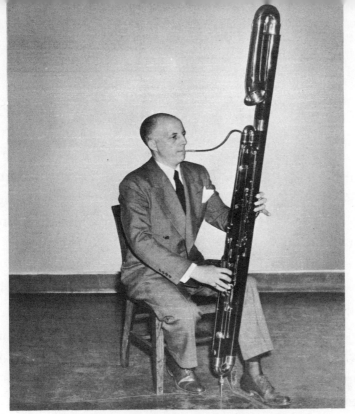

# THE CONTRA-BASSOON
## or Double Bassoon

The double bassoon or contra-bassoon is true to its name, for it is twice as long as the ordinary bassoon and sounds an octave lower. This makes the instrument sixteen feet long. A wooden tube sixteen feet long, folded several times again, really looks like a bundle of sticks! It is used mainly to supply deep tones whenever such effects are desired and it provides a solid foundation for the woodwinds just as the bass does for the string family. The contra-bassoon provides the deepest sounding notes of any instrument in the orchestra. Its range is deeper than the string bass or the tuba.

41

# THE SAXOPHONE

The saxophone, though not used regularly in the symphony orchestra, is employed occasionally in certain scores by modern composers, notably in the L'Arlesienne Suite by Bizet. It was invented by a Belgian instrument maker named Adolphe Sax about 1840, and was first introduced into French army bands in 1845. Since then it has become a most important instrument, particularly as a member of a band.

Like the clarinet it too uses a single reed mouthpiece. It is made of metal in several sizes, from the high C soprano to the low bass saxophone. This instrument is related both to the woodwind family because it is a reed instrument and to the brass family because it is made of brass.

THE SAXOPHONE

# THE BRASS FAMILY

The brass family, a most important branch of the orchestra, consists of trumpets, French horns, trombones, and tubas. The ancestry of these instruments dates back many centuries to the time when some of them were nothing more than the horn of a ram. The Bible speaks of the destruction of the walls of Jericho by means of blowing trumpets.

Instruments of this family are made of brass or nickel silver.

This group is sometimes called "brass wind" because, like the woodwinds, the player has to blow into them to produce sound. However, instead of blowing into an opening as in the flute, or into a reed as in the clarinet, he must blow into a funnel or cup-shaped mouthpiece. The early makers of these instruments discovered that the longer the tube, the more powerful and deeper the tone. Some of the instruments made were almost impossible to handle without great discomfort, for they were so long and cumbersome. By experimenting with different shapes and forms they discovered that winding or coiling these lengthy tubes made them more convenient to handle and did not interfere with the desired tone and quality. This accounts for some of the unusual shapes of the different brass instruments.

# THE TRUMPET

The trumpet is made of a narrow circular brass tube about eight feet long, coiled and folded, widening at the end to form the shape of a bell. It is exactly one half the length of the French horn. The construction of the trumpet is most intricate and there are many parts in its makeup. It has three valves which are operated by the right hand of the player. The cup-shaped mouthpiece is rather shallow. The tone of the trumpet is bright and piercing and somewhat nasal when muted. The trumpet in B flat is the one most commonly used in orchestras today. Occasional scores call for other trumpets pitched in A, C, D, etc. Wagner and some more recent composers have written parts for the bass trumpet, which is a large, deep-toned instrument.

In the average symphony orchestra three trumpets are used.


# THE CORNET

Though not a regular instrument of the orchestra, the cornet enjoys such popularity and importance in the band that it is included in this list of instruments. It is closely related to the trumpet, being an outgrowth of the old key bugle and, like the trumpet, it is a valve instrument with a tube more cone-shaped than cylindrical. The tone of the cornet is more mellow and fuller than

THE TRUMPET

that of the trumpet but not as brilliant. It is much easier to play and is a great favorite with many high school students. It is the soprano voice of the brass band and its flexible technique and lyrical quality of tone make it particularly adaptable for showy solo pieces. In the band the trumpet is secondary to the cornet and is used mainly to reinforce its weaker cousin. The cornet is often employed to play trumpet parts in smaller orchestras and has been adopted mostly by the French composers even in their symphonic writings.

## THE FRENCH HORN

This instrument owes its name to the popularity of the French Ballet in England in the eighteenth century. The horn was prominently used in the French orchestras

THE HORN SECTION

at that time, especially in hunting scenes, and the English soon began to call it the French hunting horn. This term is misleading for it is not a "French" horn and in other countries this instrument is simply called "horn."

It is made of a long tube of brass or nickel silver between 12 and 16 feet long, twisted into several circular coils, expanding into a wide bell at the end. (In all brass and wind instruments the wide end is called the bell.) The modern horn ordinarily has three valves, occasionally four, and more recently a fifth to aid in muting. These are operated by the left hand of the player. The mouthpiece of the French horn differs from that of other brass instruments in that it is funnel-shaped rather than cup-shaped. The tone of the horn is velvety and mellow, not brassy or piercing, making it one of the most expressive solo voices in the orchestra. It can be muted or softened by placing a horn mute, or the right hand of the player, in the bell.

The horn has a range of approximately four octaves and is a most important member of the orchestra. It blends well with all the other instruments and is used for solo playing much of the time. The horn generally used in orchestras is the one in F, but composers write horn parts in C, D, E flat, and almost any key. The average symphony orchestra has at least four horn players.

THE FRENCH HORN

# THE TROMBONE

The trombone is made of two brass tubes, one fitting into the other. It is called a slide trombone because one tube slides in and out of the other. This action shortens or lengthens the air column within the instrument and thereby changes the pitch, since there are no keys or valves. The trombone family was originally made in three different pitches: alto, tenor, and bass, and the trombone parts are written in these three clefs. The alto trombone, however, is now obsolete and symphony orchestras today use two tenor trombones and one bass trombone. The general range of the trombone is a little more than two octaves. Its tone is deep, rich, and full. The bass trombone is a slightly larger instrument with a larger bore and with different intervals in the slide positions.

There is also a valve trombone which does not slide but has keys like a trumpet. It is often used in bands and in some European orchestras. Its technique is much faster than the slide trombone, but its tone is not as rich. It is never used in symphony orchestras in America.

## THE TUBA

The tuba is to the brass family what the string bass is to the string family. It, also, is larger than any other member of its group, and it can play the deepest tones of all the brass instruments. The construction of this instrument, too, is rather complicated, for it is made up of many feet of brass tubing coiled and wound in different ways. It was invented by a German bandmaster named Wieprecht in 1835 and was for a long time used mainly in bands. Richard Wagner brought importance to the bass-tuba by writing for it in his operas and helped to make it a legitimate member of the symphony orchestra.

It has four valves by which pitch is controlled and uses a large cup-shaped mouthpiece. The tones of the tuba are deep and strong and it is usually used to reinforce the trombones and to furnish the bass for the brass family.

The upright tuba is used in the symphony orchestra and most concert bands while the "helicon" or "Sousaphone" is used in marching bands. The latter is a large instrument which is wound about the body of the player and extends well above his head.

THE TUBA

# PERCUSSION INSTRUMENTS

This most interesting group of instruments, often referred to as the battery, consists of the timpani, snare drum, bass drum, tambourine, Chinese drum, castanets, cymbals, triangle, tamtam or gong, xylophone, chimes or bells, celesta, and glockenspiel. They differ from one another in size, the material they are made of, and especially in the kind of sound they produce. The piano, often used in the modern symphony orchestra, must also be considered a percussion instrument because its tone is produced by a series of hammers striking against the steel strings.

Sound or tone in these instruments is produced by either rubbing one against the other, shaking, or striking them with a mallet or stick. Primitive man used drums in all kinds of festivities and religious ceremonies, for sending messages, and to instill excitement and boost morale during wars.

Of this large group only the following instruments have definite pitch: kettle drums or timpani, bells, glockenspiel, celesta, xylophone, and piano. When an instrument has definite pitch, the sound it produces can be imitated and called by its musical name. When instrument sounds cannot be imitated by whistling or singing, they are of indefinite pitch. For example: the sound a child makes by beating a pot with a spoon, the sound of a typewriter, firecrackers, a baby shaking his rattle, all these are sounds of indefinite pitch. On the other hand, sounds like church bells, factory whistles, the alarm clock, or the school bell all have definite pitch, for the sound they make can be imitated or reproduced and the notes called by their name, as D or G.

The percussion instruments of indefinite pitch are used in the orchestra mainly for rhythmical and other effects characteristic of each.

# TIMPANI
## or Kettle Drum

This instrument can be traced to the oriental countries of many centuries ago, and to all primitive people. Today it is a most important member of the symphony orchestra. The timpani is made of huge copper or brass kettles. The top of the kettle, called the head, is covered by tightly stretched calfskin. It is the only one of the drums that has definite pitch as well as the only one of the percussion instruments in which the pitch can readily be changed. This is done by means of pedals and tuning screws which tighten the head to raise the pitch and loosen it to lower the pitch.

The kind of sticks used to strike the drumhead determines the quality of the tone. The heads of the drumsticks are covered with various thicknesses of wool felt. A hard felt stick will produce rhythmical staccato and brittle sounds as well as great fortissimos or volumes of sound. A soft-headed stick will produce an entirely

## SOME PERCUSSION INSTRUMENTS
Cymbals of various sizes, Tam-Tam, Triangles, Bass Drum, Snare Drum, Chinese Drum, Tambourine, Ratchet, Castanets, Glockenspiel, Xylophone, Chimes.


## THE TIMPANI or Kettle Drum

different tone. In the symphony orchestra four or five different pairs of felt covered sticks may be used. Occasionally plain wooden sticks with small knobs are employed to produce special effects of great brilliance and volume. The kettle drums may be muted or muffled by covering a portion of the drumhead with a small piece of cloth.

It takes a player with an accurate sense of pitch and rhythm to be a good timpanist. He is very often called upon to change the pitch of his timpani several times during the playing of a composition.

The range of a pair of kettle drums is one octave. This can be increased through the addition of a higher pitched kettle drum and lowered in a similar manner. There are between two and four kettle drums in the orchestra (sometimes more) depending on the requirements of the composition.

## SNARE DRUM

The snare drum is the best known instrument in the percussion family. It resembles the toy drum with which children play in kindergarten. It has the same cylindrical shape made of wood or brass covered at each end with tightly stretched calfskin. The side on which the player beats is called the "batter head" and the lower side the "snare head." On the "snare head" side of the drum, strands of gut or steel much like violin strings are

THE SNARE DRUM

stretched across the parchment. It is the vibration of these strings against the parchment that gives this drum its distinct rattling effect. Two sticks are used to play this drum. They are made of a hard wood such as hickory and are rather thin with small wooden heads. Though the snare drum has no definite pitch, its tone is bright and vibrant, and it is used most effectively in the orchestra for rhythm emphasis. It is of great importance in bands, particularly military bands.

## THE BASS DRUM

This drum resembles the snare drum, only it is very much larger and has no snares. It comes in several different

THE BASS DRUM

sizes and is made of a wooden shell covered with calfskin which can be tightened by metal tightening rods.

The sticks used to beat this drum are rather heavy with a large head made of felt or lamb's wool which forms a soft round knob. The tone is of indefinite pitch, low, and can be either very soft or powerful.

In the orchestra this drum is used to produce special effects such as the sound of thunder in an approaching storm. It is also used to increase the volume of sound in the orchestra known as a crescendo. As a foundation for rhythm in march-like movements the bass drum is invaluable. It is this drum that supplies the very rhythmic "Boom, Boom" of our marching bands.

## THE TAMBOURINE

Mostly associated with Spanish music and dancing, the tambourine can be traced back many years to the Moorish influence in Spain. It is really a small drum made of a round wooden frame over which calfskin has been stretched very tightly. Small metal discs are inserted in this frame at certain intervals. They are inserted in pairs by means of a wire which passes through their center. The ways of playing tambourines differ. The player can strike the drumhead with his knuckles, shake the rim, or rub the head or parchment with his thumb. No matter what methods are used to play it, the bright familiar sounds are universally loved.

## THE CHINESE DRUM

Like the other drums of the percussion family this drum, too, consists of a round wooden frame, not very wide, over which painted pigskin has been stretched very tightly. It is struck by sticks with rather hard heads. Of indefinite pitch, the tone is dull, hollow, and does not carry or have very much power. In the symphony orchestra it is most effectively used to express Oriental, American Indian, and other primitive rhythm patterns.

# THE CASTANETS

The castanets were first introduced into Spain by the Moors. Like the tambourine, they are rightfully associated with Spain and her music and dancing.

Castanets are built in pairs and consist of two hollow pieces of hard wood shaped like shells. Today castanets are made of either boxwood or ebony. They are usually held in the hand and clicked together by the fingers. For their use in the orchestra castanets are mounted or fastened to a handle. The player can get the same gay fascinating rhythmic effects by shaking the handle. The dry clicking sound of the castanets is used in the orchestra to produce characteristic effects of Spanish and Latin American dance rhythm.

# THE CYMBALS

These are two round hollowed out brass plates or discs of equal size. They are held in each hand of the

THE CASTANETS

player by means of leather straps. Sound is produced by hitting the cymbals one against the other with a slight touching or scraping motion. The result of this is a very loud, bright, and powerful crashing effect. Sometimes a cymbal is suspended and struck with a mallet. This can produce either a very soft or very loud and brilliant sound of indefinite pitch. The cymbals are of Turkish origin, the country that still produces some of the very finest cymbals made today.

THE CYMBALS

# THE TRIANGLE

The triangle is made of a round piece of steel, bent so that it forms a triangle. The ends of this steel rod do not meet but are slightly open at one angle. When suspended on a gut string and struck with a short metal stick it produces a highly brilliant tinkling tone. The triangle, too, has no definite pitch.

THE TRIANGLE

THE TAM-TAM or Chinese Gong

# THE TAM-TAM
## or Gong

The Chinese are responsible for this percussion instrument and to this day the best gongs are obtained from China, Japan, or Burma. It is a wide circular plate of hammered metal resembling a huge cymbal approximately two to six feet in diameter. A soft covered stick is used to strike the tam-tam or gong, and the sound produced is brassy and low with brilliant overtones. It is often used for solemn, mysterious, and tragic effects.

61

THE XYLOPHONE

# THE XYLOPHONE

This instrument is made of bars of hard wood, arranged similarly to those of the piano keyboard. They are mounted on stretched cords in a frame. These bars vary in length and size and are each pitched in a different note. The sound of the xylophone is hard and hollow and at times brilliant. The tones are produced by striking the wooden bars with hard sticks or mallets. The range of this instrument is between three and four octaves.

# CHIMES
## or Bells

Chimes are circular metal pipes of shiny brass, generally nickel plated, about one inch in diameter and from four to six feet long. They are suspended from a bar in a metal frame by means of a heavy string. There are between eight and thirteen chimes in a full set. They are struck near the top with a rawhide mallet and the tone produced is brilliant yet solemn or festive, similar to that made by our church bells.

THE CHIMES or Bells

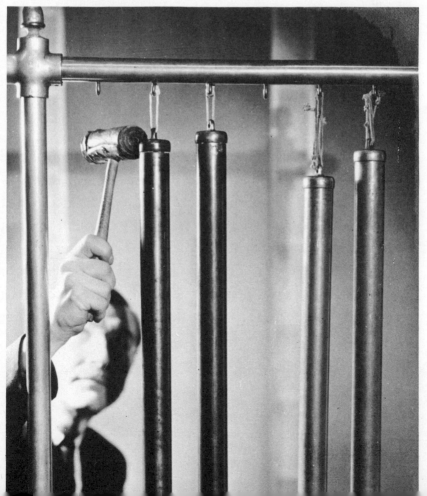

# THE CELESTA

The celesta is a comparative newcomer to the orchestra. In looks it resembles a small upright piano and it is played in a similar manner. Hammers like those of the piano strike tuned steel plates, producing a pleasant bell-like tinkling tone. A good example of this instrument's sound can be found in the "Dance of the Sugar Plum Fairy" from Tchaikowsky's Nutcracker Suite. Tchaikowsky introduced the celesta to the orchestra when he first heard it in Paris in 1891 in the workshop of its inventor, Victor Mustel. He was greatly impressed by its sweet beauty of tone and delicate quality and promptly wrote a piece for it in his Nutcracker Suite, which had not yet been completed.

# GLOCKENSPIEL
## or Orchestra Bells

This instrument looks like a small xylophone. The bars, however, which are also arranged like a piano keyboard, are made of polished steel instead of wood. Small mallets of hard or soft rubber are used to strike the bars, which produce a sweet and tinkling tone of definite pitch.

In the orchestra the bells are used particularly to create special ethereal effects and are heard often in the works of Wagner, Tschaikowsky, Debussy, and other composers.

THE CELESTA

THE GLOCKENSPIEL or Orchestra Bells

# 3

# On Choosing an Instrument

NOT TOO LONG AGO the boy seen carrying a violin or other musical instrument was often supposed to become a professional musician. People looked at him as if he were very different, and his classmates felt strange towards him for he seldom participated in after-school activities and had little time for anything but practice and lessons. Today the picture is entirely changed. Music is recognized as a most important factor in everyone's life regardless of special musical ability.

There are now more opportunities for young people to learn to play a musical instrument than ever before. In many schools teachers are employed to teach band and orchestra instruments and in large cities fine teachers of these instruments are to be found who teach privately and also in community and settlement centers.

The greater number of the boys and girls who take advantage of these opportunities do not wish to make music their profession. Instead they find that it is a lot of fun to play in the school orchestras and bands and to meet with other people who love to play. They also discover that playing a musical instrument is a fine way to earn money while in school. One fifteen-year-old girl obtained all of her spending money playing the piano for a dancing class every Friday after school. Many high school boys and girls have been able to earn money playing for school and church parties, and numerous students are earning their way through college playing musical instruments.

Band and orchestra instruments require various physical abilities of the player. Unfortunately not enough people pay much attention to the aptitudes required and many select instruments to learn for which they are not at all suited. One ten-year-old boy had a friend who was learning to play the trumpet. He immediately decided that that was the instrument he wanted to play. His parents, convinced of his interest, bought the instrument without consulting anyone to find out if their son had the features required for playing the trumpet. The teacher they selected tried to discourage his taking lessons. His lips and teeth were not those that would permit the best results on this instrument. The boy and his parents insisted but, after six months, all of them decided that lessons on another instrument would be advisable. Since this boy had a good ear and excellent rhythm, his teacher recommended the study of percussion instruments, and because of his strong long fingers and wide hand-span the piano or a string instrument was also considered.

Mistakes in the selection of an instrument are costly. The price of the instrument, lessons, and music is bad enough, but worst of all is the discouragement, after spending much time and effort, of being completely unsuccessful. The music teachers, orchestra members, soloists, and conductors of the future are the girls and boys learning to play musical instruments today. We cannot afford to have them make mistakes, even beginning ones.

I. Choosing the instrument

    1.    The person who can be of the greatest assistance in deciding on the right instrument is the teacher who plays and teaches this particular instrument. He will know the physical needs and requirements and should be the first person to consult.

    2.    The school band or orchestra leader is another person who can help in this decision.

    3.    The teacher or music supervisor at school will have a good idea as to ability and aptitudes and can also be of great assistance.

II. Age most suitable for beginning music lessons on various instruments

    1.    The age at which to start taking music lessons depends upon the interest and upon the instrument selected. A child of five or six years of age can start lessons on the piano, or even the violin, and make fine progress. Should he want

to learn to play a wind or brass instrument, however, he could not possibly do it because his physical development would not permit it, no matter how interested he might be.

Because it is almost impossible to know the instrument best suited for very young children and because the piano does not have too many limitations, it is an ideal instrument with which to start. Everyone will gain much from piano lessons and the training will prove invaluable as general background for any other instrument. *Before attempting lessons on any of the orchestral instruments one should be at least nine years old.*

III. Physical and other requirements necessary to play musical instruments

1. To play a string instrument such as the violin, viola, violoncello, string bass, and the harp it is a great help if the student has strong straight fingers and a large hand-span. Even with these qualifications there will be a limitation of age. For instance, no one can play the string bass unless he is at least able to reach the strings and support the instrument. This means that the child must be at least thirteen years of age or over.

2. Students attempting to play an instrument with a cup-shaped mouthpiece like the trumpet or trombone should have straight even teeth and

strong lip muscles. Protruding teeth would be a hindrance in playing these instruments.

3. The lips are another factor to consider. Thin lips are best suited for playing instruments with small mouthpieces like the trumpet or the French horn.

4. For playing reed instruments, especially the English horn and the oboe, the teeth should be straight, not too long, and the lips not too heavy. It is also advisable to have some experience playing another reed instrument before attempting to play one of these; the clarinet is recommended.

5. To play the bassoon, long strong fingers are a great help and, in addition, the player should have lips that are not too heavy and teeth that are even.

6. To play larger instruments like the bassoon, trombone, and string bass the pupil should be at least of average size and weight and have hands, lips, and teeth suitable for the playing of these instruments.

7. The French horn requires more than average musical talent and ability as well as a sensitive lip, a good ear, straight teeth, and previous training on another brass instrument, if possible. It is a very difficult instrument to learn to play and only those really interested and willing to work especially hard should attempt it.

THE CLARINET FAMILY, Bass Clarinet in center.

8. Requirements for playing the trombone are a good sense of pitch as well as of touch, for even slight variations in moving the slide will produce tones either flat or sharp.

9. The clarinet and the cornet can be played more easily than most of the other band and orchestra instruments. The clarinet especially has practically no physical limitations. Both instruments need only an interest and a willingness to learn.

10. In order to play such instruments as the tuba, French horn, and the trumpet, lung power should be taken into consideration, for it takes a great deal of blowing to sustain sound.

11. To play the timpani, one must be something of a super-man! The timpani player is usually expected to play all the instruments of the percussion family. Though so many girls and boys feel that it is a simple thing to learn to play them, the requirements are very rigid. A timpanist must have almost perfect pitch, an excellent sense of rhythm, plus good muscular coordination. The snare drum is the best of this group on which to start lessons. This should be followed by the study of xylophone and bells before undertaking the study of tympani.

To learn to play the snare drum, one should not be over fourteen or fifteen years of age, because later certain muscles are more set and necessary manipulation of the drumsticks will be harder to master.

IV. Buying your instrument

1. Someone who knows instruments well should be consulted before buying an instrument. The teacher of the instrument would again be of great assistance here.

2. An instrument should be bought only from a reputable dealer. If a music store carrying a good selection is not available, manufacturers should be requested to send catalogues giving all the information and prices. The addresses of the instrument manufacturers can be obtained from advertisements in music magazines. The school and public library can be of assistance in getting these addresses.

3. An instrument should be bought on approval. Most firms and individuals will permit the prospective buyer to have the instrument for several days' trial.

4. Used instruments are perfectly all right, if very carefully checked by someone who knows instruments.

V. Finding a teacher

1. For orchestra and band instruments, the best teacher is the person who plays the instrument professionally.

2. In places where there is no available instruction for certain instruments and where commuting

is impossible, a child can teach himself to some extent by means of instruction books. Most of the good music publishing houses have methods for teaching various instruments at home. Occasional supervision by a well trained musician is necessary, however.

It is becoming more and more the usual thing for girls and boys to learn to play an instrument. Those interested should not be discouraged by the limitations imposed, for in spite of them, most people have the aptitude to play one instrument, and often more. The most important thing is to take advantage of the opportunity to learn to play and to be interested in hearing and making good music.

There are now at least 25 major symphony orchestras in the United States consisting of 65 to 110 men, and hundreds of amateur and semi-professional orchestras. New orchestras are being formed constantly and those in existence are growing in size, artistry, and importance in the communities which support them. Music is an ever important factor in our education and culture. Today the American musician has more and greater opportunities to further his career than ever before. A wide field of employment exists in symphony orchestras and bands, in teaching positions in schools and colleges, and in the concert field for those who excel in solo work. With all these developments and with the American composers writing and having their works performed by all of our great orchestras, the future of a recognized American musical culture seems very bright and hopeful indeed.

# 4

# Practice Makes Perfect

THERE ISN'T a girl or boy who expects to learn to swim, play tennis or hockey without actually working at his particular sport. Yet, many of the same girls and boys will start music lessons and expect to make progress with very little practicing, if any. Anything new to be learned requires concentration and at least some work. This is especially true in learning to play the piano or any other musical instrument.

Though habits, needs, and schedules differ, some of the following suggestions for practicing may prove helpful.

1. *Practice must be a daily routine* and no days should be skipped during which the instrument is neglected. If a work period must be omitted, it should not be the one right after the lesson. It has been found from experience that practice immediately after teaching is of the greatest benefit because at this time one is

most likely to remember the teacher's corrections and suggestions.

2. *A definite time for daily work is a great help.* A short practice period of twenty minutes before school in the morning, when one is refreshed by a good night's rest, will accomplish more than spending the same time at the instrument later in the day. Beginners under seven or eight years of age will find that thirty minutes a day is sufficient time in which to prepare their lessons. These thirty minutes might even be divided into two fifteen-minute periods. The more advanced student will require more time at his instrument because his assignments will be longer and more difficult. Most pupils find that their lessons can be well prepared if they practice carefully for one hour a day. Even for the older pupil, the hour period may be divided into two thirty-minute sessions.

3. Readiness for practicing is also important. All music should be gathered beforehand so that it will not be necessary to waste time hunting for the next selection. Practice should not be interrupted or disturbed by other activities. Instructions and suggestions made by the teacher during the previous lesson should be followed as closely as possible. There is always a good reason for having to hold the instrument a certain way and for having to use only certain fingers in playing!

4. In learning a new composition, play the whole work through as carefully as possible. This will give an idea of the problems and difficulties the selection presents, as well as a general musical feeling for it. The pupil can

THE HARP

next divide it into sections or parts and work on one portion at a time. It is not a good idea to work on the full assignment the first day after the lesson. One piece should be finished to perfection before beginning the next. Assignments such as scales and exercises should be practiced daily.

Some girls and boys have found that a carefully worked out practice schedule is of great help to them. One eleven-year-old boy seemed to have such a hard time settling down to practice. His parents were always urging him to do his work and usually his reply was "later." He was persuaded to work out a schedule and both he and his family are much happier about it. His schedule, which is pinned up in his room, has a duplicate in the kitchen. This is an exact copy of it:

| | | |
|---|---|---|
| Monday ....8:00- 8:30 A.M. | 5:30-6:00 P.M. | After school free |
| Tuesday ....8:00- 8:30 A.M. | 7:30-8:00 P.M. | |
| Wednesday ...8:00- 8:30 A.M. | 5:30-6:00 P.M. | |
| Thursday ............... | 7:30-8:30 P.M. | Boy Scouts after school |
| Friday ......8:00- 8:30 A.M. | Lesson 5:00 P.M. | After school free |
| Saturday ....9:30-10:30 A.M. | | |
| Sunday...No practice if Friday lesson is excellent. | | |

Because this boy lives close to his school he is able to get almost half of his practicing done before school starts.

Whatever one's practice schedule may be, the important thing to remember is that twenty minutes of good concentrated effort is far more worthwhile than an hour that is carelessly spent.

For beginners and for very young children it is

advisable that the parent or some other older person supervise the practice period. This will help form good practice habits and will avoid waste of valuable time. The parent will find that the time spent practicing with the child will be amply rewarded in his correct playing, progress, and musical understanding.

# 5

# Building
# a Home Record Library

ANYONE WHO has never had a phonograph and records
to play has no idea what a joy they can be. It is as if one
were endowed with super-human powers to be able to
command performances of the very best orchestras and
soloists who never tire nor complain no matter how many
times they are asked to perform.

Building a record library is similar to building a
library of books. It is much more difficult, however, to
select the best in records than it is in books. The librarian,
so capable and willing to guide in the selection of books,
has no parallel when it comes to buying records. Too often
it is difficult to know which recording to buy for there
may be three or four recordings or even more of one particular work. This, however, offers no real barrier and
should not prevent anyone from starting a record library.

Though the first records bought ought to be those
with which one is already familiar, the wise record col-

lector does not fill his library with those works only. It is best to include an occasional unfamiliar work even if the first hearing seems a little strange.

The best way to judge whether a recording is worth buying and adding to a library is to consider how well it will stand constant repetition. Some popular works sound wonderful at the first hearing and one is tempted to buy them immediately but, after they are played five or six times, they become extremely uninteresting. Great works will seem to improve with every hearing and be ever fresh.

In general, a good record collection should not be too one-sided. Some musicians like to specialize in opera or chamber music or symphonic works, but for most people a wider selection is best. This should include not only the best examples of works of different composers but many different forms in music as well. Such a collection can be an education and a constant joy to its possessor. Most composers wrote in all forms of music. Some specialized in symphonies like Mahler and Sibelius, some in opera like Verdi and Wagner, and some wrote mainly piano music like Chopin. But most of them, like Beethoven and Mozart, wrote symphonies, chamber music, concertos, sonatas for different instruments, vocal music and opera. An interest in hearing different compositions by many composers will develop into a better understanding and a greater general knowledge of music and will result in a record collection of lasting value.

The following list is suggested as an aid in the selection of records. From it special favorites may have been omitted. Any one of the works included will make a fine start or will be a good addition to a record library already established. In music, as in books, there are immortal classics which nobody should miss. Their appeal is universal and they have no age limits. This list is by no means complete, for it is impossible to prepare any one list of records to fit the needs, likes, and interest of all young people.

## SOME RECORD SUGGESTIONS FOR A BEGINNER'S LIBRARY

BACH, JOHANN SEBASTIAN
Concerto No. 2 in E major for violin
Concerto in D minor for two violins
Suite No. 2 in B minor for flute and strings
Suite No. 3 in D major

BEETHOVEN, LUDWIG VAN
Concerto No. 5 in E flat major (*Emperor*)
String Quartet No. 7, Op. 59, No. 1
Symphony No. 5 in C minor
Symphony No. 6 in F major

BIZET, GEORGES
Excerpts from the Opera "Carmen"

BRAHMS, JOHANNES
Academic Festival Overture
Hungarian Dances
Symphony No. 1 in C minor
Symphony No. 4 in E minor

COPLAND, AARON
Appalachian Spring

DEBUSSY, CLAUDE
  The Children's Corner Suite
  Afternoon of a Faun

DE FALLA, MANUEL
  El Amor Brujo
  The Three Cornered Hat: Dances

DUKAS, PAUL
  The Sorcerer's Apprentice

DVORAK, ANTONIN
  Symphony No. 5 in E minor
    (*From the New World*)

ENESCO, GEORGES
  Roumanian Rhapsodies Nos. 1 and 2

FRANCK, CESAR
  Symphony in D minor

GRIEG, EDVARD
  Suites from Peer Gynt

HANDEL, GEORGE FREDERICK
  Water Music

HAYDN, FRANZ JOSEPH
  Symphony No. 94 in G major (*Surprise*)
  Symphony No. 101 in D major (*Clock*)

HUMPERDINCK, ENGELBERT
  Opera "Hansel and Gretel"

MENDELSSOHN, FELIX
  Symphony No. 4 in A major (*Italian*)
  Fingal's Cave Overture
  Midsummer Night's Dream Music

MOZART, WOLFGANG AMADEUS
  Symphony No. 41 in C major (*Jupiter*)
  Serenade *"Eine Kleine Nachtmusik"*

PROKOFIEFF, SERGE
  Symphony No. 1 in D major (*Classical*)

PUCCINI, GIACOMO
Opera "La Boheme"

RACHMANINOFF, SERGE
Piano Concerto No. 2 in C minor

RAVEL, MAURICE
Bolero
Mother Goose Suite

RIMSKY-KORSAKOFF, NICHOLAS A.
Capriccio Espagnol
Scheherazade

SAINT-SAENS, CHARLES CAMILLE
Carnival of the Animals
Danse Macabre

SCHUBERT, FRANZ PETER
Ballet Music from *"Rosamunde"*
Symphony No. 8 in B minor (*Unfinished*)

SCHUMANN, ROBERT
Scenes of Childhood for Piano
Symphony No. 1 in B flat major

SIBELIUS, JEAN
Symphony No. 2 in D major
Valse Triste, Swan of Tuanela, Finlandia

SMETANA, BEDRICH
The Moldau

STRAVINSKY, IGOR
Petrouchka
Fire Bird Suite

STRAUSS, RICHARD
Till Eulenspiegel's Merry Pranks
Don Quixote

TSCHAIKOWSKY, PETER ILICH
Symphony No. 6 in B minor (*Pathetique*)

Nutcracker Suite
Piano Concerto No. 1 in B flat minor

WAGNER, RICHARD
Overtures
Selections from Operas
A Siegfried Idyll

Record suggestions for younger boys and girls to help them recognize instruments of the orchestra and to give them an introduction to some of the composers. No one would want or need all of them for his collection. It is, therefore, recommended that they be heard and the selection made according to the interest and need.

Instruments of the Orchestra
(2-10" Cabot 4021)

Pan the Piper, Tubby the Tuba,
Peter and the Wolf
(Columbia CL 671)

Britten, Benj. Young Person's
Guide to the Orchestra
(Columbia ML-5183)

There are a number of very good recordings based on the lives and music of classical composers, of which the Vox listings are here presented. However, two other series are worthy of consideration. These are: "Life, Times, Music" series issued by Period Recordings and "Story Told to Young People" produced by Atlas Recordings.

| Bach: | His Story and His Music | (Vox MM 3500) |
|---|---|---|
| Beethoven: | "    "    "    "    " | (Vox MM 3600) |
| Berlioz: | "    "    "    "    " | (Vox MM 3640) |
| Brahms: | "    "    "    "    " | (Vox MM 3580) |
| Chopin: | "    "    "    "    " | (Vox MM 3520) |
| Foster: | "    "    "    "    " | (Vox MM 3620) |

| | | | | | | | |
|---|---|---|---|---|---|---|---|
| Grieg: | His | Story | and | His | Music | | (*Vox MM 3550*) |
| Handel: | " | " | " | " | " | | (*Vox MM 3560*) |
| Haydn: | " | " | " | " | " | | (*Vox MM 3610*) |
| Liszt: | " | " | " | " | " | | (*Vox MM 3630*) |
| Mendelssohn: | " | " | " | " | " | | (*Vox MM 3530*) |
| Mozart: | " | " | " | " | " | | (*Vox MM 3510*) |
| Paganini: | " | " | " | " | " | | (*Vox MM 3630*) |
| Rossini: | " | " | " | " | " | | (*Vox MM 3650*) |
| Schubert: | " | " | " | " | " | | (*Vox MM 3540*) |
| Schumann: | " | " | " | " | " | | (*Vox MM 3550*) |
| Sousa: | " | " | " | " | " | | (*Vox MM 3620*) |
| Strauss, J: | " | " | " | " | " | | (*Vox MM 3590*) |
| Tschaikowsky: | " | " | " | " | " | | (*Vox MM 3570*) |
| Wagner: | " | " | " | " | " | | (*Vox MM 3660*) |

# 6

# Famous Makers
# of String Instruments

THERE IS something strangely mysterious about the old
makers of string instruments. The more one reads about
them and the more one studies their instruments the
greater seems to be the mystery. For many years instrument makers all over the world have been trying to find
the formula which made it possible for these men to produce the wonderful instruments which are so highly
prized today, but thus far they have not been able to
do so. It is almost as if they signed a pact to take their
secret with them when they died.

Some instrument makers of today feel that this
secret lay in the varnish and the way it was applied; some
think that it was in the choice of wood used; and another
theory prevalent is that the instruments, having been
played constantly for so many years, have simply aged
and mellowed with time. At any rate, for more than three
hundred and fifty years the violins, violas, violoncellos,

and double basses that these instrument makers produced have been perfect examples of the art of violin making and modern makers have not been able to create instruments to equal them. Their dimensions, design, and construction have been copied exactly but to no avail. Excellent and highly priced instruments have been built by many modern instrument makers, but somehow the mellowness, brilliance, and quality of tone that are at once evident in an old master, are usually missing to some extent in the modern reproductions.

It was in a little town of Brescia, Lombardy, that the first modern string instruments were made over three hundred and fifty years ago. Gasparo Bertolotti, known as da Salo after the place of his birth on Lake Garda, in Italy, may well be called the father of the modern violin. A well known and excellent craftsman, he became dissatisfied with the existing instruments, the viols. No matter how carefully he worked and how hard he tried, the tone they produced was small with little or no brilliance. Though he had never heard instruments with bigger and more brilliant tones, he still felt that such instruments could be made.

With his pupil Giovanni Paolo Maggini, he set out to build a new kind of instrument that would have the big brilliant tone we now have in the modern violin. After many experiments and hard work, the two craftsmen created a model, not too far removed from the viol family, which had the qualities he was seeking. Soon the news of the instruments made by da Salo and Maggini spread all over Italy and their model was copied by other makers. Some kept the exact proportions and specifications of these instruments, while others made some minor changes in them. They still had much in common with their immediate ancestors, the viols, but their strings were reduced and unified to a standard four, they were less cumbersome and more simple in design, and had the bigness of tone and the brilliance, especially in the violin and the violoncello, that Gasparo da Salo wanted so much to hear. It is as if these violin makers could look into the future and foresee the great genius of the composers who would be writing music for strings that would require the perfect instrument we know today. Long before violinists like Paganini were in need of as fine an instrument as his own violin made by Joseph Guarnerius, these instruments were there, ready for them. They must have known that the artistic and technical achievements of the great concert performers to be, like Kreisler, Heifetz, and countless others, would require the brilliant instruments they made then.

It is interesting to note that though most of the fine instruments were copied from the original Gasparo da Salo model, they all differ in many details. Each violin maker was an artist in his own right, and added something to his instruments to distinguish them from those of other makers. Most of the old Italian masters made all of the instruments of the string quartet, violins, violas, violoncellos, and basses, yet each had his specialty. Some of them are especially famous for their violins, others for violas or violoncellos. Gasparo da Salo made all of the string instruments, yet, of all his creations, the violas are the most prized and are considered his best. Not all instruments of this period are equal in value even though they bear the name of a famous violin maker. Violins made by Antonio Stradivari have sold for as high as $40,000 or more, while those made by Nicolo Amati sell for about $7,500. Many other makes of old Italian instruments sell for very much less.

Though the first and the finest of the modern string instruments were made in Italy, other countries, too, have produced some fine craftsmen in this field. It is true none of them have created instruments quite as fine as those of the Amati or the Stradivari family. Nevertheless, a large number of the instruments which appeared many years later are excellent and are highly valued. The large number of string players, and the very high prices of the old Italian instruments, make it impossible for many musicians to own an old authentic Italian instrument. A great many performers use instruments made in France, Germany, Czechoslovakia, and America and find them adequate. In most orchestras the concertmaster usually has a fine Italian instrument because of the large number of solos he is called upon to play. Many of the leaders of the string sections of the orchestra, such as the first viola, violoncello, and bass also usually have fine instruments but the majority of the players use an instrument of a lesser known Italian maker, or of a much later period, or one made in another country.

In looking over the names of the great Italian string instrument makers, it is not unusual to find several makers with the same name. This is so because it was the custom for sons to follow the trade of their fathers. A son did not always produce work as fine as that of his father but often the instruments made by a son or a grandson far surpassed those made by the father or grandfather. As an example, the greatest of the Amati family was Nicolo, who was the grandson of Andrea Amati, the first violin maker of the family. Both his father Girolamo and his uncle Antonio, as well as his grandfather and his own son Girolamo, were famous instrument makers in Cremona, but it is the work of Nicolo Amati that is much superior to that of the others.

The following is a brief list of some of the better known Italian instrument makers. It is by no means complete and the dates of birth and death are in many cases only approximate.

**Amati, Andrea  (1535-1581)**

He was the founder of the Cremona school of violin making. His two sons, a grandson, and a great-grandson followed his trade and produced some very fine instruments. The best known of the Amati family is Nicolo, grandson of Andrea.

**Bergonzi, Carlo  (1683-1747)**

He was one of the best pupils of Stradivari, and it is believed that he took over his business after the death of his sons, Francesco and Omobono Stradivari. Michel Angelo Bergonzi (1722-1765) was not as fine a craftsman as his father, Carlo, and Nicolo Bergonzi, who worked in Cremona about 1760-1796, was better than his father, Michel Angelo, but not as good as his grandfather, Carlo.

## Gagliano, Alexander (1660-1725)

Eight members of this family made string instruments and produced some very fine ones. Alexander and Nicolo are considered the very best craftsmen. The Gagliano violoncellos are the best of the instruments they made.

## Gasparo da Salo (Bertolotti) (1542-1609)

Founder of the Brescian school of violin making, creator of the modern violin as we find it today. Violas made by this maker are considered particularly good.

## Goffriller, Matteo

Worked in Venice about 1690-1742. Though not of Italian birth he and his brother, Francesco, learned the art of violin making there, producing many fine instruments, of which the violoncellos are particularly prized.

## Guadagnini, Lorenzo (1695-1750)

He worked with his son, Giovanni Baptista, who is the best known member of the family, and his two grandsons, Giuseppe (Joseph) and Gaetano I, made some beautiful instruments of which the violoncellos are particularly fine.

## Guarnerius, Andreas (1626-1698)

He is the first of a large family of instrument makers in Cremona, a pupil of Nicolo Amati. His sons, Petrus and Giuseppe (Joseph), worked with him and learned much

THE STRING FAMILY
Double Bass, Violoncello, Viola, Violin, Viola d'Amore reclining.

about the art of making fine instruments. It is Joseph (Del Gesu) Guarnerius, his nephew, who is the most celebrated member of this family and is considered, next to Stradivari, the finest violin maker. Petrus Guarnerius II, the son of Joseph (Del Gesu), was also a fine craftsman though not quite as good as his father.

### Landolfi, Carlo Ferdinando

He worked in Milan, Italy, about 1734-1788 with his son, Pietro Antonio, to whom he taught his trade. The instruments made by the father are considered superior to those made by the son.

### Maggini, Giovanni Paolo (1580-1632)

He was an apprentice of Gasparo da Salo and helped in the development of the modern string instruments. He developed his own style in later years and produced some excellent instruments.

### Montagnana, Dominicus (1690-1750)

He was a worthy member of the Venetian school of violin making. His instruments are very fine and very highly priced.

### Rogeri, Giovanni Battista (1650-1730)

He and his son, Pietro Giacomo, were both pupils of Nicolo Amati. The work of the father, who also made some basses, is superior to that of his son.

### Ruggeri, Franciscus (1620-1694)

He is the oldest and most important member of his family. As pupil of Nicolo Amati, he had much to teach to his own two sons, Giancinto Giovanni Battista and Vincenzo.

Storioni, Lorenzo  (1751-after  1801)

The last of the great craftsmen of the Cremonese school,

Stradivari,  Antonio  (1644-1737)

He mastered the art of violin making to produce some of the very best instruments, surpassing those of his teacher, Nicolo Amati. His sons, Francesco and Omobono, were his pupils, and though they made some wonderful instruments, it is their father who is considered the greatest of all instrument makers.

Tecchler,  David  (1666-?)

Worked in Rome, Italy, about 1705-1743. His violoncellos are the best of the instruments he made and rank very high.

Testore,  Carlo  Giuseppe  (1660-1717)

He and his two sons, Carlo Antonio and Paolo Antonio, worked in Milan and produced a large number of good instruments.

# PICTURE CREDITS

*Pictures are of members of the Cleveland Symphony Orchestra and their conductor, George Szell. Two members of the NBC Orchestra staff of Hollywood, California were photographed with the saxophone, bass drum, xylophone, cymbals, triangle, and celesta.*